THE

LITTLE

MARINER

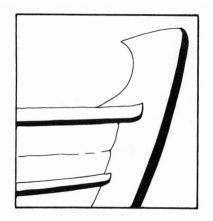

Port Townsend

ODYSSEAS ELYTIS

The Little Mariner

TRANSLATED BY OLGA BROUMAS

with a preface by Carolyn Forché

Copper Canyon Press

Portions of this translation have appeared in *The Agni Review, The American Voice, The American Poetry Review,* and *The Poughkeepsie Review.*

ISBN 1-55659-014-8
Library of Congress Catalog Card Number : 87-72467

The Greek publisher of the original text is Ikaros Books.

The publication of this book was supported by a grant from
the National Endowment for the Arts.

Copper Canyon Press is in residence with Centrum at Fort Worden State Park.

The cover is from a photograph by Gerasimos Steris,
courtesy of Ikaros Press.

The type is Palatino, set by Fjord Press Typography.

Book manufactured by McNaughton & Gunn.

COPPER CANYON PRESS
P.O. Box 271, Port Townsend, Washington 98368

Preface:

AN APPRECIATION

After several years of being less than a faithful servant of
my art, I approach a poetry such as Elytis has written and
Broumas has brought into English with gratitude that such
apokatastasis remains possible. To describe those years, I re-
trieve one line from an earlier Elytis poem: *War and war and not
one rag to hide deep in our things and forget.* It had been my
intention to know the world as if it were apart from myself,
and to become more fully conscious, as if consciousness were
a repository of experience and wisdom, rather than an analog
of the world itself.

"In consciousness," as Julian Jaynes has written, "we are
always seeing our vicarial selves as the main figure in the
stories of our lives." But we are never less conscious of the
world than when we perceive ourselves thus, and we are
never more ignorant of life, perhaps, than when we are most
convinced of our awareness. It is often by sheer accrual of
experience that we become so convinced. When we set out on
a journey, we are most fortunate when we arrive where we
began, as Elytis has done in the voyage of *The Little Mariner*
and as he has helped me to do, in returning me to the homeland of my soul's youth. Mine was far from Greece, from its
whitewashed walls rinsed with light, its olive groves, its sea
radiance. My soul was born to snowfields and iced lakes, fac-
tory smoke and in summer, the drone of beetles in the false
wheat.

"Like the hungry knead bread in their sleep," I read *The Little Mariner*, after six years of exile from poetry itself; and although any poet might have brought me back, it was Elytis, through Broumas, who did so. It is my pleasure to retrace his path again and again, so as to commit to memory the journey's progression.

Upon entering *The Little Mariner* we are provided an itinerary. We enter through longing: *Gold wind of life why don't you reach us?* The first of four spotlights shines onto the dark proscenium of human history, illuminating scenes in which human beings suffer injustices and betrayals. We then "bless the best" of the world in the twenty-eight prose poems entitled "Anoint the Ariston." "With Light and with Death," we proceed through twenty-one lyric passages obsessed with light, the sea floor, justice, the sea, the concept of generosity, the girl, the concept of nakedness and Greece itself.

The "bare necessities" for such a journey are provided in a travel sack of "What one loves," from the Attic Greek *otto tis eratai*: passages of poetry and music, still lives, grave stelae, engravings and portraits, friezes and sonatas, concertos, icons, wall paintings and ideas. We have with us Aeschylos' "far-flung wanderings," Dante's *"Lo bel pianeta che d'amar conforta,"* El Greco's "Left view of 'Jesus on the Mount of Olives,' " Yeats' "the moonless midnight of trees," that we might also be possessed of them, to diminish our impoverishment. We are even, where necessary, told where to find these possessions: in which museums and private collections, in what cities and countries. As we open and admire each of Elytis' gifts, we are moved to assemble one day just such a travel sack of our own.

But now we are going, and among those with us are Matisse, Baudelaire, Rothko, Braque and Éluard. The spotlight illumines again scenes of human injustice. We witness these tableaux, linked by their common horrors, "simply," as Terrence Des Pres has written, "to keep watch over life." Our purpose is not to redeem the past but to remind ourselves of it. Again we "Anoint the Ariston," again bless the best: the *blue-blooded storms, this wooden table with tomatoes and olives, alphabets, aromatic grasses, rough cambric sheets, the whitewash on the wall, bird dew, basil breezes,* all of which Elytis has grown fond of and at one with, *St. Prekla's sill among wild figs, scorched land, abandoned chapels* and *vineyards asleep like children.*

"With Light and with Death," we are carried again, in pure, unparaphraseable lyric utterance and in several Greek languages and forms: Sapphic Greek as if erased by time, island and mountain Greek, the Greek which survived five hundred years of Ottoman occupation, Byzantine Greek and vernacular Greek, both the demotic (of everyday speech) and the formal *katharevousa*. It is a tribute to Olga Broumas' abilities as a translator that so many Greek languages find their equivalencies in contemporary English. Each word, whether antiquated or colloquial, seems preserved in the rarity particular to its utterance, honoring Elytis' desire "... to create [words] exactly and only in this manner. From then on, the analogy between the phonetic composition of words and the material content they are called to give to phenomena seems to have the inevitable character of Fate or of primary physical elements."

Perhaps in Broumas' hands, Elytis has found the best transposition of his work into English. A native of Greece who spent her entire youth and adolescence there, she is not only fluently bilingual, but of the two worlds created by Greek and English, and a poet of Elytis' own tradition as far back as Sappho. In another translator's hands, Broumas' rendering of *War and war and not one rag to hide deep in our things and forget* became *Wars occurred and recurred, and not even a rag was left to hide deep within our things and forget it.* In Broumas' translation we are trusted to cross through the poems safely and close to the Greek, without a syntactical scaffold to assure our balance.

We have now returned again to "What One Loves," and this time we enter the Aegeodrome (an homage to the Aegean, at once the creator and creation of Greek). It is from this luminous pelago of language, turbulent, radiant and in flux, that consciousness surfaces to bring the world into being. In Elytis' cosmology, language creates the world. In the Aegeodrome, we find his words, the vocabulary of a particular soul, the words and what they call into being, among them *anemone, bergamot, cardamom, dovecot, eucalyptus, foam, ghost, hurricane, isthmus, jib, kiss, licorice, mistral, naranja, olive, parapet, quince, ravine, salt, tassel, unspoken, vineyard, wave, yard,* and *zephyr.*

"No maps or anything, just words. But words leading precisely to what I searched for."

Again, given time, we might make our own such spatial construction of loved words, but the spotlight is shining once more, further along in Greece's history, where "The first Christian King, Constantine, orders his own son, Krispos, arrested and put to death." Betrayal follows betrayal and we aren't permitted to avert our eyes, lest we mistake our purpose: "to recompose the world, literally and metaphorically, so that the more its desires are realized, the more they contribute to the materialization of a Good accepted by all humans." We must not avert our eyes, and yet he has elsewhere cautioned poets to guard against "competing with events and giving over to horror, rather than balancing it" with light, form, and the response of conscience.

For we are involved here with "a metaphysics where the phenomenon of language is not the sum of a few words/symbols for things, just as landscape is not simply the sum of some trees and mountains, but a complex signifier, an ethical power mobilized by the human mind, precursing things." And it is through this ethical power that we have the ability "to recompose the world."

We have returned to bless what is best. *That I wanted good poetry without knowing it . . .* (Milosz) and ". . . the special courage Poetry gave me: to be wind for the kite and kite for the wind, even when the sky is missing," to understand "the meaning of a celestial body whose light is our assimilated labor." This was the wisdom needed through the years of *War and war and not one rag to hide deep in our things and forget,* and perhaps this from "Anoint the Ariston": that "Doubtlessly a separate, irreplaceable sensation exists for each of us, which if we don't find and isolate in time, and cohabit with later, and fill with visible acts, we're lost."

"With Light and with Death," we journey forward again (and in my personal journey come serendipitously to the lines *You St. Salvador, who dress in storms / Raise the sea's eye and let me travel*) to the acknowledgment of death, ours and the death of others, of the betrayed, of the victims of injustice, of those we loved. In the weeks following such a death, I come with great relief to this poetry of consolation: that *Even when they destroy you it will still be beautiful / The world because of you / your heart – true heart / In place of what they took from us –* You who are now *in the second / homeland of the upper world.*

Departing that homeland, we return to "What One Loves," once more to *fill with visible acts* that "irreplaceable sensation." We have entered a gallery of snapshots, moments so precisely focused, so lovingly developed, that "having existed once, nothing ever again could abolish" them. *Eleven o'clock, wind on the uphill to old Chora. Not a soul.*

The last spotlight illumines the nineteenth and twentieth centuries in Greece and Cyprus; in its final tableau, a national leader "just manages to escape." But he does escape, and once again we "Anoint the Ariston": *Yes, Paradise wasn't nostalgia. Nor, much less, a reward. It was a right.* It was within. "The poet's 'I'," Elytis has written, ". . . is not the poet as he is formed in the world; it is the world as it is formed in the poet." We have come to the beginning of our journey, longing for the *Gold wind of life* . . .

This is a poetry of luminosity and resonance, clarity of soul, and deep transformative power. It cannot be imitated. Such work arises out of the language itself, and such a language out of the sea, the rocks, the history and light of Greece, but arises only if such a poet as Elytis is present, and occurs in English only when a translator such as Broumas emerges to assimilate his labor.

Carolyn Forché

PROVINCETOWN
DECEMBER, 1987

THE

LITTLE

MARINER

CONTENTS

SOMETIMES IT'S NOTHING BUT
   a flash behind the mountains – there, by the island-littered sea. Sometimes again a strong wind suddenly stops outside the harbors. And those who understand grow tearful

   Gold wind of life why don't you reach us?

No one hears, no one. Everyone walks with an icon, and on it, fire. And not a day, a moment in this place without injustice, murder

   Why don't you reach us?

I said I'll leave. Now. With whatever: travel sack on my shoulder; guidebook in my pocket; camera in hand. I'll go deep in the soil and deep in my body to find out who I am. What I give, what I am given, and still injustice has the greater part

   Gold wind of life . . .

THE

LITTLE

MARINER

[*Spotlight a*]

SCENE ONE : Open-air court in the ancient city of Athens. The accused arrive and proceed among curses and cries of Death! Death!

SCENE TWO : A jail in the same city, beneath the Acropolis, walls half-eaten by dampness. On the ground, a miserly straw mat and in the corner, an earthenware jar of water. On the outside wall, a shadow: the guard.

SCENE THREE : Constantinople. In the harem of the Holy Palace, in candlelight, the Queen throws a pouch of gold coins to the Head Eunuch who bows and looks at her significantly. By the open door, his men at the ready.

SCENE FOUR : Drawing room of a large Monastery. Oblong table, the abbot at its head. Sweaty monks come and go bringing news: a crowd spills into the streets, setting fires, destroying everything.

SCENE FIVE : Nauplio. Greek and Bavarian officers outside the King's quarters converse in low tones. A messenger takes the dispatch and heads toward the steps that lead on high to Palamidi.

SCENE SIX : In front of an old and empty lot in contemporary Athens, a crowd, motley with priests and bishops, gathers to cast a stone, "the stone of anathema."

SCENE SEVEN : Low buildings of EAT/ESA. In the courtyard, drunk soldiers. Braying and lewd posturing. The officer leaving some cell says something to the military doctor. Behind them thuds and cries are heard.

ANOINT THE

ARISTON

[I–VII]

I

ONE DAY, in the devoted eyes of a young calf, I found again
the life I'd lost. I understood I was not born in vain. I started
picking through my days, rummaging, searching. I wanted to
palpate the matter of emotions. To restore, from the hints
I found dispersed throughout this world, an innocence so
powerful it washed out blood – injustice – and forced people
to my liking.

Difficult – but how else? Sometimes I feel I am so many I get
lost. I want to be realized, even along the length of a lifetime
exceeding mine.

If even time can't conquer lies, I've lost the game.

I I

I INHABITED a country emerging from the other, the real one, as dream does from my life's events. I called it Greece as well and drew it on paper to keep it in sight. So slight it seemed; so vulnerable.

Time passed, I kept testing it: with sudden earthquakes, blue-blooded storms. I'd change the place of things to rid them of all value. I studied the Sleepless, the Monastic, to learn the making of brown hills, small Monasteries, fountains. I even laid out a whole garden of citrus fragrant with Heracleitos, Archilochos. The fragrance frightened me, it was so much. So, gradually, I took to binding words like jewels, to cover the country I loved. Lest anyone see the beauty. Or even suspect it isn't there.

III

ROAMING my country in this way I found its slightness so natural I said, impossible, this wooden table with tomatoes and olives by the window must have purpose. So that this sensation, extracted from the wooden square with its few vivid reds and many blacks, can lead directly to iconography. And it, reciprocal, must in a blissful light extend over the sea until the slight's true grandeur is revealed.

I am afraid to speak in arguments belonging by all rights to spring; but only then do I embrace the virginity I profess, and only so imagine her keeping her secret virtue: by rendering useless all the means contrived to maintain and renew her.

I V

I DIDN'T find spring in the fields or, even, in a Botticelli, but in a small red Palm-bearer. Likewise one day, gazing at a head of Zeus, I felt the sea.

When we discover the secret relationships of meanings and traverse them deeply we'll emerge in another sort of clearing that is Poetry. And Poetry is always single as the sky. The question is from where one sees the sky.

I have seen it from midsea.

V

I WANT to be as truthful as the white shirt on my back; and straight, parallel to the lines of country-house and dovecot, which are not straight at all and for this reason stand so certain in God's palm.

With all my pores I lean toward a – how to say? – spinning, awesome *good*. From how I bite into a fruit to how I look out of a window, I feel a whole alphabet take shape, which I try to activate with the intent of joining words or phrases, and the ulterior aspiration, iambs, tetrameters. Which means: to conceive and speak of another, second world that's always first in me. I can even call a host of insignificant things to witness: storm-ridged pebbles, streams with a comfort in their roll, aromatic grasses, bloodhounds of our sanctity. An entire literature inhabits the human soul – ancient Greeks and Latins, the later historians and lyrics; an art, the Well-known, the Full Moon: all can be found there transliterated and stenographed by the smooth, the fresh, the rigorous and the ecstatic, which is their only genuine and authentic reference.

This soul I call innocence. And this chimera my right.

VI

OH YES, a truly healthy thought – regardless of its reference
– endures the open air. And not only that. In our sensitivity it
also must be summer.

A little cooler, two or three degrees, it's done: the jasmine
shuts up, sky becomes noise.

VII

SMILE, bitter lip, my second soul!

WITH LIGHT

& WITH DEATH

[1–7]

1

I turned death's face to me like an oversized heliotrope
The cove of Adramytenos appeared with the mistral's curly
            spread
A bird immobilized between sky, earth and the mountains
Lightly placed one in the other. The child who ignites
Letters now came running to bring back injustice to my chest
My chest where Greece the second of the upper world
            appears.

These things I say and write so no one else may grasp –
As a plant is content with its poison until the wind
Turns it to fragrance in the earth's four corners –
Will later appear in my bones phosphorescing a blue
The Archangel carries dripping from his arms with huge
Steps fording Greece the second of the upper world.

2

Since falling in love with these small bodies I grew thin, transparent. Asleep, awake, I thought of nothing else but how to raise them, one day to bed them. I hid behind doors. Learned to catch them in water, wind. I still don't know what to call them.

A – White or cyanic, depending on the hour and placement of
    stars.

B – Really wet. A pebble.

Γ – The lightest; your inability to pronounce it betrays the
    degree of your barbarity.

P – Childlike and in fact, almost always, of female gender.

E – All wind. The sea breeze takes it.

Y – The most Greek letter. An urn.

Σ – A pest. But a Greek must occasionally whistle.

3

You're young – I know – and there's nothing.
People, nations, freedoms, nothing.
But *you are*. And while you
Leave by one foot you arrive with the other
Torn by love's light
With or without your will
Piper of plants you come gathering the idols
Against us. Long as your voice lasts.

How when you touch the virgin's cricket
The muscles pulse under your skin
Or how animals who drink then gaze
Erase misery: like you
Take thunder from the Gods
And the world obeys. Go then
Spring depends on you. Accelerate lightning

Grab SHOULD by its d and skin it to its s.

4

I wait for the hour when a
Merciful garden will assimilate
The centuries' outcasts – when a
Girl will declare on her body beautiful
Revolution with trembling voices and pyrotechnic
Fruit returning history
To *go*
     and then
Even the Franks might Hellenize
Arriving at the fig tree's liver
Or taking dictation in their sleep
On the perfection of surf
       and through a mental fissure
The exhalation of some brave
Lavender first met in childhood
Might appease the angry astral space.

Three hours' walk outside memory I found myself hunting
in the vowel forest. A marksman by instinct (and sentimental)
I shoot and bring down:

emblem	May	vial
line	sea	captain
halcyon	oranges	jewel
prey	fountain	dazzling
murmur	tassel	Syrtis
only	gnosis	Marina
mint	metallic	Miletos
rhythm	filter	silver
shrine	deliberate	herald
little	mother-of-god	Monastery
mandarin	pleat	Myrtilla
Pergamos	stellar	blossoming
belt	high noon	languid
sunflowers	fields	March
oracle	morning	cube
mystic	flora	spout

clearing

6

What do you want, what are you after
                    where is the meaning fallen from your hands
The music only you hear and the nude
Feet changing earth like a dancer
Who snaps the comet of her hair and a spark
Falls there before you on the rug
Where you see truth betray you

Where do you go, what sorrow, what flaming
Dress rends your flesh, what restored
Ancient fountain meaning to make you oracular
Like this, leaf by leaf, pebble by pebble

Teenager kneeling on the diaphanous seafloor
Whom the more I sleep and dream the more I see
Rising with a basket of seaweed and green shells
Biting the sea like a coin, the same sea who
Gave you brilliance, this light, this meaning you seek.

Now that the mind is forbidden and the hours don't
Circulate from garden to garden my thought
Shy as a first-time rose bush
Clinging to the gate
Tries to reconstruct
With darts of brilliant dew
Those age-old greens and golds that in us
Always think it's July seventeenth
So St. Marina's water on the stones again might be
Heard, the fragrant-with-embracing-couple sleep,
The voice
        a voice like Mother's
And barefoot on the Mesolonghi flagstones
Freedom come walk again
As when the poet greeted her – blessed be his
        hour – in our name
And we've had Easter since.

WHAT ONE

LOVES

[*The Travel Sack*]

I emptied and refilled my travel sack. "The bare necessities,"
I said. And they were plenty for this life – for many more. I
started, one by one, to write them down:

CRETE
Engraved stone seal with representation of chamois
(*Heraklion Museum*).
The Prince of Lilies (*Knossos*).

THERA
Kore (*Wall painting*).

EGYPT
Portrait of a woman (*Ouserat Grave, no.* 51).
Youth with Antelope (*Menna Grave no.* 69).

HOMER
dusky water
brightly burnished interiors
then an ineffable ether was cleft from the sky

ARCHILOCHOS
the souls of waves in their embrace

SAPPHO
many-eyed night

HERACLEITOS
Extinguish hubris not fire
Child's is the kingdom

PINDAR
all equally falsely swim to shore

cold flame

search large Quiet's brilliant light

ETRURIA

Young men restraining horse (*Tarkynia*).

Piper among birds (*Three-bed Grave*).

ATHENS

By Euphronius: Leagros Mounted (*Monaco Museum of Ancient Art*).

Team of riders from the Parthenon frieze.

Small Aphrodite Statue (*Berlin Museum*).

Aphrodite with flexed legs (*Rhodes Museum*).

Prostitute guarding the grave (*National Archaeological Museum*).

Amynokleia (*Grave stele*).

AESCHYLOS

far-flung wanderings

inky sun-struck race

surf's countless mirth

SOPHOCLES

rains a fresh mist of tears

Sleep, innocent of pain

for you I call eternal sleep

BYZANTIUM

Passage from the "City of Nazaret" (*Kachrieh Mosque*).

Palm-bearer from the Capella Palatina (*Palermo*).

Manuscript by Iakovos Kokkinovafos: Paradise. Its gate and four rivers (*Bibliotèque Nationale de Paris*).

Passage from the "Presentation of the Virgin" by Michael Damaskenos (*Byzantine Museum, Athens*).

Saint Demetrios. Folk icon of the Macedonian School (*Private Collection*).

ANASTASIOS
We all burn in tears

ROMANOS
even my blood black,   where I dip and write
sweetening flower   became a weed to me

DAMASCENOS
in ageless youth
Funereal Mass
O my sweet spring

DANTE
Lo bel pianeta che d'amar conforta
E come giga e arpa, in tempra tesa
di molte corde, fa dolce tintinno

PAOLO UCCELLO
The battle of San Romano (*National Gallery, London*).

FRA ANGELICO
Left view of the "Coronation of the Virgin" (*Louvre Museum*).

PIERO DELLA FRANCESCA
La Natività (*National Gallery, London*).
Fragment from the "Whipping" (*Galleria Nazionale delle Marche, Urbino*).

EL GRECO
Left view of "Jesus on the Mount of Olive Groves" (*Museum of Art, Toledo, Ohio*).

VERMEER
The Atelier (*Vienna, Federal Museum*).
The Music Lesson (*Buckingham Palace*).
The Sleeper (*Metropolitan Museum, New York*).

VIVALDI
Concerto C-dur für Piccolo Blockflöte, Streicher und Cembalo, P. 79.
Largo from the Concerto D-moll für Viola d'amore, Streicher und basso continuo, P. 266.

BACH
Suite number 2 for flute and strings (1067).
Concerto in F, for oboe, strings and continuo (1053).

HAYDN
Trio in A H.X.V. number 18.

MOZART
Divertimento in E-flat major for violin, viola and violoncello, K. 563.
Allegro from the Concerto for piano and orchestra no. 15 in B-flat major, K. 450.
Andante from the Concerto for piano and orchestra no. 21 in C major, K. 467.

BLAKE
wash the dusk with silver

BEETHOVEN

Sonata for violin and piano no. 2 in A major, opus 12.

Sonata for violoncello and piano no. 5 in D major,

opus 102, 1.

HÖLDERLIN

Ein Räthsel ist Reinentsprungenes. Auch

Der Gesang kaum darf es enthüllen

Denn schwer ist zu tragen

Das Unglück, aber schwerer das Glück

NOVALIS

Sie wissen nicht, dass du es bist der des zarten Mädchens

Busen umschwebt und zum Himmel den Schoss macht

Jahrtausende zogen abwärts in die Ferne, wie Ungewitter

KALVOS

circle-chased sun

and the pelago gets rich

from the smell

of golden quince

SOLOMOS

for some affairs of the soul

And him in the multi-stellar ether

The turtle-dove's lament she murmured in her sleep

NERVAL

Mon front est rouge encore du baiser de la Reine

MALLARMÉ

Et j'ai cru voir la fée au chapeau de clarté

PAPADIAMANTES
of the aged oak, who by the cymbal petals of its leafbearing
limbs narrates the centuries' memoirs.
Then, through the open window, I saw a star shine
in the interior of the small house.

RIMBAUD
Je pisse vers le cieux bruns, très haut et très loin,
Avec l'assentiment des grands héliotropes.

KAVAFIS
In the month Aithyr   Leukios went to sleep
a Mrs. Irene Andronikos Assan

YEATS
the moonless midnight of trees

BAUDELAIRE
Nous aurons des lits pleins d'odeurs legères
L'homme y passe à travers des forêts de symboles

MATISSE
Still Life with Oysters (1940; *Kunstmuseum, Basel*).
The Plum Branch (*Private Collection*).
Grey and Blue Cutout (*Éditions Verve*).

KLEE
The Goldfish (1925–26; *Private Collection, Holland*).
Tracks of Aquatic Plant (*Lyonel Feininger Collection*).

PICASSO
Horse in Circus. Drawing (*The Museum of Modern Art, New
York*).

Woman with Fan (*Averell Harriman Collection*).
Woman, Child and Seahorse. Drawing (*Musée d'Antibes*).

BRAQUE
Still Life (1934; *Kunstmuseum, Basel*).

JUAN GRIS
Banyuls' Bottle (*Herman Rupf Collection, Berne*).
Still Life with Roses (*Private Collection, Paris*).

ARP
Enak's Tears (1917; *Private Collection*).
Torso with Flowering Head (*Private Collection*).

ÉLUARD
Une sublime chaleur bleue
D'une écriture d'algues solaires

LORCA
Silencio de cal y mirto

UNGARETTI
Astri Penelopi innumeri

EZRA POUND
you are violets with wind above them

DALÍ
Nostalgic Echo (*Private Collection*).

ROTHKO
Untitled (1951; *Mr. Gifford Phillips Collection, New York*).

THEODORAKIS
The Myrtle
In the secret cove
Gloria from the *Axion Esti*

HATZIDAKES
Birds
A Virgin Mary

MOUSTAKI
The Emigré

G. GUSTIN – M. TÉZÉ
Monsieur Cannibale

THE

LITTLE

MARINER

[*Spotlight b*]

SCENE ONE : Bedridden, with a gangrenous leg, Miltiades has been transported to the court and there, with surprise and ultimate despair, hears his condemnation.

SCENE TWO : Patiently, after his ostracism by the Athenians, Aristeides boards the boat that will take him from his land.

SCENE THREE : Pheidias, thrown in jail like a criminal, dies slowly of old age and sorrow.

SCENE FOUR : The forces mobilized by the Thirty plunder and massacre.

SCENE FIVE : After his condemnation, on a pauper's mat, in jail, Socrates, calm, drinks the hemlock and releases his soul.

SCENE SIX : Alexander the Great, standing outside his tent, orders the execution of his devoted General Parmenion.

SCENE SEVEN : In a general melee, Phokion and his friends, not allowed to defend themselves, are sentenced to death.

ANOINT THE

ARISTON

[VIII – XIV]

VIII

NAKED, JULY, high noon. In a narrow bed, between rough cambric sheets, cheek on my arm I lick and taste its salt.

I look at the whitewash on the wall of my small room. A little higher is the ceiling with the beams. Lower, the trunk where I have set all my belongings: two pairs of pants, four shirts, white underclothes. Next to them, the chair with the huge matting. On the floor, on the white and black tiles, my two sandals. I also have by my side a book.

I was born to have so much. Paradox doesn't interest me. From the least you get anywhere faster. Only it is more difficult. You can get there as well from the girl you love if you know to touch her, and then nature obeys you. And from nature too – if you know to remove her thorn.

I X

"YESTERDAY I thrust my hand under the sand and held hers. All afternoon then the geraniums looked at me from the courtyards with meaning. The boats, those pulled to land, took on something known, familiar. And at night, late, when I removed her earrings to kiss her as I want to, with my back against the stone church wall, the pelago thundered and the Saints came with candles to give me light."

Doubtlessly a separate, irreplaceable sensation exists for each of us, which if we don't find and isolate in time, and cohabit with later, and fill with visible acts, we're lost.

X

WHATEVER I was able to acquire in my life by way of acts visible to all, that is, to win my own transparency, I owe to a kind of special courage Poetry gave me: to be wind for the kite and kite for the wind, even when the sky is missing.

I'm not playing with words. I mean the movement you discover being written in an "instant," when you can open it and make it last. When, in fact, Sorrow becomes Grace and Grace Angel; Joy Alone and Sister Joy

with white, long pleats over the void,

a void full of bird dew, basil breeze and a hiss of resonant Paradise.

X I

FANTASTIC TRUTHS perish slower. Rimbaud survived communism as Sappho's moon will survive the moon of Armstrong. Different computations are necessary.

The clock we face doesn't count hours but doles out imperishability and waste, in which we partake either way, as we partake of youth or age. Perhaps for this reason, I was always less afraid of death than illness; and a tender body dazzled me more than a tender sentiment.

The sun explodes in us and we stand, palm to mouth, terrified.

The wind is up. The sacred triumphs.

XII

FROM THE PEBBLE to the fig leaf and from the fig leaf to the pomegranate, as from the Kouros to the Charioteer and from the Charioteer to Athena.

I dream an Ethics whose final reduction leads to the same consubstantial and indivisible Triad.

XIII

HOMER'S SHORES harbored a bliss, a majesty, that reach unaltered to our time. Our feet, gouging the same sand, feel it. We walk, thousands of years, the wind incessantly bows the reeds, and we incessantly raise our faces. To where? Till when? Who governs?

We need a legal code that develops like our skin during our growing years. Something both youthful and strong, like the ancients' *in water everlasting* or *weep blossoming tears*. So what we humans birth might surpass without oppressing us.

XIV

I COMPLETED my higher mathematics in the School of the sea. Witness some exemplary sums:

(1) If you deconstruct Greece, you will in the end see an olive tree, a grape vine, and a boat remain. That is: with as much, you reconstruct her.

(2) The multiplication of aromatic grasses by innocence always gives the shape of some Jesus Christ.

(3) Happiness is the correct relationship between deeds (forms) and emotions (colors). Our life can be cut, and has a duty to be cut, to the dimensions of Matisse's colored papers.

(4) Wherever there are fig trees there is Greece. Wherever the mountain rises above its word there is a poet. Bliss is not subtractable.

(5) An evening in the Aegean is comprised of joy and sorrow in such equal doses only truth remains in the end.

(6) Every progress in the ethical plane must be inversely proportional to the ability of power and numbers to dictate our fate.

(7) A "Departed" for half of us is, by necessity, a "Revenant" for the other half.

WITH LIGHT

& WITH DEATH

[8–14]

As in   in a kiss' eon
I can't catch you Fate
            I you liv   in shade
      hammer   cheekstone in the veins
                        where points the masthead alw
            birched the sky a peacock
Rays with white the top clouds   on the hill
One   Green gold and leafiness of bird that
Gazes at water through the reeds
                        uninhabited soul from
Solitary swallow you brought me a tear.
                                    now
            mourning
With fresh arg   cave that just broke
And ha
                                    of old trees
Dreams incl   as island by waves   and there
At shore's edge
Smeared Ethiopianlike with Moon   high
                        homeless families of stars and maps
That angels draw with an invisible right
Hyp   ra   as always.

Have you ever thought of it,
The grape, at the hour when love shapes you
As time shapes the stalactite? And the orange, have you
Seen it stirring in your dreams
Once Maria – twice young moon
The foliage all still dark
And heavy with death too slow to scatter?

What does it mean
To be from a good family as the cricket from a fir ax
How equally meaningless and ready for loss
And ready for duration in golden time are you?

Child – you dare call me! Play if you dare
Pretend me a plant – wrap me a wind
Enter a virgin's sleep and bring her dress
In your teeth like a dog. Or if not, then
Bark, bark, behind your shadow
As I have, a whole life, inside high noon.

10

I speak with the patience of a tree that rises
In front of a window as old as it
Whose shutters are eaten by the wind
Who keeps pushing it open and keeps wetting

With Helen's water and with words
Lost in the dictionaries of Atlantis
One I – and from the other side the Earth
Side of destruction and of death.

The tree that knows me says "hold on"
It gathers clouds and keeps them company
As I keep to white paper and to pen
On nights that have no clock to see

The meaning of "you shouldn't," "it's not right."
I have seen virgins, I have opened
Their downy shell to find the inner
Side of destruction and of death.

LUCKHALFKILLTHEOTHERHALFFORYOU
GREEKSCOMESAYOUNGDAUGHTERWITHS
UNFLOWERINHANDASKINGFORJUSTICE
ANDNEVERSHOWINGWHICHMOUNTAINLI
NEINHEROPENPALMISAROADWITHWIND
INTHEHAIRANDVOICEOFWATERSSEATH
ECANISTERTHATNOFOREIGNERIMAGIN
ESHELPINGWITHFILLSWITHHISTHUND
ERALWAYSALONETHEONETREATEDUNJU
STLYASTHESPRINGUNDERTHESTONEOF
FATHERSUNTILFINALLYONTHEHOURYO
UWILLSPILLWITHFORCEOCLEARLIGHT

Just for a moment play on your guitar
The names of the Virgin and you'll see

Hey hey Golden-haired
Hey hey Golden-staired

The mountain leap again a white house on its flank
The two-winged horse
And the sea's wild strawberry you'll see

My Luminous my Channel and my By-the-door

The green boat bob and vanish in the cornrow surf
And Mitsos with the hair and little chain around his neck

Hey Lady of the Well
Hey Virgin So Much Water

Curse and raise unsuspecting in his nets
Four or five ancient Greek
A *téllesthe* and a *neusí*, a *mélea* and *krínai* like

Karystian and Kleidian
Daphnian and Argeian

Just for a moment play them on guitar
And from the burning pelago out front you hear

Hey Crystalline hey Morning Dew
Hey Virgin of the Victors

The scrim of sky being torn in two
And an ancient adolescent identical to you
Descending – look:
Upright atop the waves with a harpoon and on the white foam
        floating

Cave-dweller Myrtle-limbed Sea-going hey!

13

They're always safe in me
At anyone's disposal: the lunging but immobile
North boulder
The solitude of sacred surf
And the infernal sleep four times
More powerful with a Zeus all its own thundering
On an invisible white beach.

Signs in the air: zeta – eta – omega
(High at the hour when down deep
A foaming Sikinos goes by)
Perpetually transmit that pain
Rings falsely in the body
And danger – you need but be a strong
Helmsman or a Kite
        to quickly pin him.

14

To Beauty, to Mary, the bipolar star
Who holds a dove and her hand shines.

WHAT ONE

LOVES

[Aegeodrome]

When I opened my guidebook I understood. No maps or anything. Just words. But words leading precisely to what I searched for. And slowly, turning the pages, I saw space being shaped like a tear by deep emotion. And I inside.

agape	bluefish
Alexandra	bluefly
All Soul's day	boat
anchor	bolt
anemone	bougainvillea
Anna	boulder
ant	braided rug
arch	bride
arm in arm	brine
armoire	butterfly
aspen	
astringent	café
August	cage
	caique
bait	canary
barbette	candle
barrel	candlestick
basil	cape
basket	captain
bay leaf	cardamom
beach	cardinal
beam-reach	castle
beeswax	caulking
bell	cemetery
bergamot	chameleon
birdsong	chamomile
bitter sea	chapel
blanket	chicken coop
blueing	cicada

cistern
citrus
Claire
clear sailing
cliffs
clockwork
colored pebbles
cool wind
cobblestone
comb
cork
cove
crab
cricket
crops
cross
cuttlefish
cyclamen
cypress

dandelion
daphne
deckhand
desert island
dogwood
dolphin
donkey
dovecot
doublemint
dragnet
dry
drystone
dumb

East wind
easy
echo
eggplant
Eleni
embers
eucalyptus
exile

fair
fallen olives
farmer's cheese
fern
feta
fiancée
fig
filter
firefly
fireplace
fish hook
fish soup
fisherman
fishing lights
fishing line
fishing net
flag
flashlight
florins
flower water
flowerpot
foam
fortune telling
fountain
frankincense

frappe

fresh

Froso

frost

funeral walk

garfish

geranium

ghost

girl

glare

goat

gooseberry

grandma

grape

grass

gull

gust

halter

hare

harpoon

hedge

heliotrope

high ceiling

high sea

holy water

honeycake

honeysuckle

horse of the Virgin

hurricane

hyacinth

hydrangea

hyssop

icon

incense

Indian fig

isthmus

ivy

jar

jasmine

jib

jujube

jumping-jacks

June

July

keel

kerchief

kilns

kiss

lament

lampblack

lapping

latch

lavender

lemon tree

licorice

light-hearted

lighthouse

light-shadowed

lily of the shore

limpet

little bell

little stairs

lizard

lobster
locust
loom
low wall
luff

mad
magic
Mall
mandarin
Mando
marble
Marina
marzipan
mast
mastic
mat
medusa
melon
memorial
mint
mistral
monastery
moon
mooring
morning joy
moss
motorboat
muleteer
mullet
muscat
must
myrrh
Myrtle

naranja
nettles
noon
Northeasterly
North wind

oars
ochre
octopus
offering
oil lamp
oil press
old man
olive
omelet
orange
oregano
Orion
ouzo
oven
ozier

pail
Palm Week
pampas
parapet
pass
pebble
pelago
perch
perpendicular
petal
pew
philodendron

phylactery

pine

pine resin

pinna

pistachio

pitch

pitcher

plane tree

plank

Pleiades

plum

poppy

port

prime

promise

prow

psalter

pumice

quail

quince

radishes

rascal

ravine

red earth

red lead

red mullet

resin

rope

rose

rose bush

rosemary

rowlock

ruins

saddle

sails

salt

salutations

sandstone

St. Mamas

Sta. Monica

Sta. Paraskevi

Sti. Anargyri

schooner

scorpion

sea

sea-bird

sea-breeze

sea cave

sea floor

sea urchin

seal

seaweed

seine

September

sesame

shack

sheepskin

shell

shrimp

shroud

silvered

sirocco

sister

sleep

slip

small bridge	unspoken water
smallfry	
source	vessel
Sou'westerly	veteran
sparrow	vine leaves
spinning wheel	vines
spright	vineyard
squall	viper
stalactite	virgin
starfish	
starlight	wash
stern	watermelon
stone ship	watersquash
stone sill	wave
storm	weed
strait	well water
such	Westerly
sun	whitefish
swallow	whitewash
swordfish	wild cherry
	wild dove
tassel	wild goat
Taxiarch	wild pear
tent	wind
terraced	windmill
three-masted	woodbind
threshing ground	woven
tiller	
tillia	yard
tomato	
turpentine	zephyr
turtle dove	zucchini

THE

LITTLE

MARINER

[*Spotlight c*]

SCENE ONE : The first Christian King, Constantine, orders his own son, Krispos, arrested and put to death.

SCENE TWO : Heracleios's men have led his nephew Theodoros and his illegitimate son Adalarichos to the torture chamber. They cut off their nose, hands and right foot.

SCENE THREE : Having blinded her minor son Constantine, Irene the Athenian proclaims the Eunuch Stavrakios Grand Justice.

SCENE FOUR : Theophano secretly leads her lover Ioannis Tsimiskis to the matrimonial chambers of the Palace so he can murder Nikiforos Phokas.

SCENE FIVE : Inside the church, during the memorial service for Emperor Theodoros Laskaris, Michael Palaiologos murders the minor Ioannis IV and takes his place.

SCENE SIX : During Christmas matins Michael Travlos, aided by six other conspirators, kills his benefactor Emperor Leon V.

SCENE SEVEN : Andronikos Komnenos strangles his nephew Alexios and marries his widow who is thirteen years old.

ANOINT THE

ARISTON

[XV–XXI]

XV

MY CHILDHOOD YEARS are full of reeds. I spent a lot of wind growing up. But only so did I learn to separate the slightest whispers, to speak precisely among the mysteries.

A language like Greek where *agape* is one thing and *eros* another; desire one thing and longing-with-a-beating-heart another; bitterness one thing and marasmus another; guts one, entrails something else. In clear tones I mean which are – alas – grasped less and less by those who more and more are distanced from the meaning of a celestial body whose light is our assimilated labor, just as it doesn't cease revolving every day, all brilliance, to reward us.

Whether we want to or not, we are the matter as well as the instrument of a perpetual exchange between what sustains us and what we give it to sustain us: the black we give to receive white, the mortal, everlasting.

And we're indebted to some bright duration for our potential joy.

XVI

THE SOUL too has its dust, and woe if the wind doesn't stir in us. Urges beat down our windows, glass shatters. Few know the emotional superlative is formed of light, not force. That a caress is needed where a knife is laid. That a dormitory with the secret agreement of bodies follows us everywhere referring us to the holy without condescension.

Ah! when time comes to sit on some St. Prekla's sill among wild figs, red-fruited mulberries, in an abandoned place, a jagged shore, then little Button, candle in her hand, will reach on tiptoe for the flammables inside our sigh: spites, passions, cries of rage, ten thousand confetti insects brightening the place.

XVII

AND THERE, in the midst of misery, from Santorini's excavations, from beyond despair – at last: a Kore Therasia comes proffering her hand as if to say "Greetings O Graced."

I am no painter, Kore Therasia. But I will tell you with whitewash and with sea. Extend you by my writing and my acts. Offer you a life (the life I didn't get) without policemen, without files, or cells. A white bird just above your head.

I'll plant vineyards – words. Build Palaces with what you give me to love. I'll go from Hegeso to St. Ecaterine. I'll bring earth and peace.

XVIII

THEY FILLED my head since childhood with the image of a death hooded in black, who brings life like a trap and holds it open, baited with bliss. Let me laugh. Who chewed the laurel said otherwise. And it's no accident we all orbit the sun.

The body knows.

XIX

HI, Beautiful Archangel, blisses like fruit in a pan!

XX

A MOUNTAIN of wildflowers, wiltless and unchanged as in
our thought, trembles each time we manage to turn to air.
And to think that, provided we all wanted to, we *can*. As we
can span the endless acres of ethics that extend beyond the
single and abominable – alas – one, where a most ancient
stupidity transfixes us in its almighty endurance.

XXI

I EXPRESS MYSELF as a bergamot in the morning air. The filtration no one else perceives is what counts. Through social struggle, through the yearning for justice and freedom, through man's inalienables: an aroma!

A person is never as large or small as the meanings he grasps, from the Angel to the Demon. It's like the space left when these two rival forces self-destruct. If it pleases me to refer to a tree's nobility or turn answers to riddles, it's for this: to understudy the child I was and have again on hand, entirely for free, that endless visibility, the mightiest, most enduring of Revolutions.

I was looking at what fit the large square window: some scorched land, a stripe of deep blue surf. Later, in my sleep, three in the afternoon, I saw Hermes descending from the sky, leg flexed, holding a small girl in his arms, head upside down, her hair poured in the wind.

WITH LIGHT

& WITH DEATH

[15–21]

15

This stone head and broken flowerpots
Setting like the sun at the hour of irrigation
In Aegina or Mytilene – this fragrance
Of jasmine lemon-balm and hyssop
Keeping the sky at a distance
If you really are the one
That moment passing high over the rooftops
Just like a schooner with open sail

The girls' songs full of earth
Where tears shine like Ursa Major
And the abundant sky-grass you set foot on
Once, and once and for all exists
Annexed to your own Greek state
If you really are the one who lives and lives against
Superfluous things and days
The Jesus on the left O
                              then you will understand me.

16

Where shall I speak it, night, in the wind
Among the loquat stars, in the blackness reeking
Of sea, where speak the Greek of bitterness
In capital trees, where write it so
The wise will know to decipher
Between the second and third wave
Such heavy burning mood of stones that didn't sink

You, St. Salvador, who dress in storms
Raise the sea's eye and let me travel
Miles in its green transparence
To where the masons excavate the sky
And find again that moment before birth
When violets filled the air and I knew not
That thunder knows nothing of its flash
But strikes you thrice – all light!

As in the sky in spring
Gray-green you appeared
Winnowing a rain of myriad rays

And walking toward a slippery slope
Of stars with a flask of sleep you
Evaporated having trampled

The idle-tongued.
The mountains were veiled by armies
Of crystalline frankincense

And not to be outdone night's
Poppies bloomed until
Thousand-winged

Words from your lips
Restored now wholly
The once grasped dreams

Of mariners.
Like a goatherd's solitary lantern you
Lit our soul in the abyss, Kore.

18

Even when they destroy you it will still be beautiful
The world because of you
                        your heart – true heart
In place of what they took from us –
Will still beat and a gratitude
From the trees you touched will cover us

Unshackled lightning how do they retie you

Now that I have no air no animal companion
Nor even a woodsman's lost thunderbolt
I hear water running
                        maybe from God
(And I blaspheming) or from the mouth
Of a solitary who approached the peak's most Secret Keys
And opened them
                        for this I address You
Night of a Holy Tuesday with the irreplaceable pelago
Facing me – so you can tell it goodbye and thanks.

19

The trotting of good horses will help me
Say my prayers before sleeping
On a mat – as I was born – with a little spittle
Of sun on my forehead and my ancient heart
Who has all of Homer and so still endures

Pounding exhaustively in the black stone
Of Psara a worshipful light
I bring you future Greek
Daisies who have put a candied almond in Hell

I tell with courage of the little gold
Atop the gates like the birds know
To leave an idea of joy and then die

Hi there my faucet open drop by drop
Again fills azure time

Who is innocent and has no count.

20

You were saying I should leave yesterday the most
Lacerated sea we took the candelabrum
With the thirteen blue Myrtle-twigs I am
or even if you come a roof with legible below it

On your body Homer's words
Surfward reflections
Airy Poseidon all carnations
Of signs because fresh I was until.

21

And most important: you will die.
The other Horn-head will open
A mouth for you to enter, your face white
While even the music will continue and on the trees
Which you never turned to see, the frost will be dismissing
Your works one by one. So what?
                                        Think now
Whether truth generates
Raindrops, whether the galaxy expands
In fact, then wet, glowing, with your hand
Atop a noble laurel you'll depart more Greek
Than I who blew you prime winds in the strait
Who packed whitewash and tempera in all your luggage
The little icon with its gold Julys and Augusts   .
You knowing all along when I'd be
Lost, on foot, you'd take me in
Lifting onto the tablecloth
The bread the olives and the conscience
Our first day in the second homeland of the upper world.

WHAT ONE

LOVES

[*The Snapshots*]

Above all, precision, I would say. And take care to keep the f-stop narrow. When I started developing I saw it clearly: I'd wrested types from moments which, having existed once, nothing ever again could abolish.

a

KERKYRA
Spring night in a distant country graveyard. That luminous cloud of fireflies that lightly shifts from grave to grave.

MYTILENE
At Mystegna, morning, climbing the olive groves to the chapel of Sta. Marina. You feel a weight subtracted like sin or remorse, and digested by the coarse soil as if drawn by magnanimous ancestors.

SKIATHOS
Just as the small boat meets the sea-cave, and suddenly, from the awesome light, you are enclosed in frozen blue-green mint.

ANDROS
Strapourgies. Moonlight on blossoming ravines all the way to the fragrant unending pelago.

MYKONOS
Small terrace. Between pots of geraniums, a rose dome, white arrows, masts weaving the sky, Delos.

PAROS
"Eletas" farm. Twilight. Ducks and geese. Someone on the threshing floor, asleep, a huge straw hat on his head, his legs half parted.

KYTHNOS
Spine of the island "Pepper," asymmetrically triangular as twilight approaches from Kanala.

SERIPHOS
Sailing along the island at high noon. Your nude arms burn on the prow. The small embraces keep unfolding, one from the other, until at last the great one opens out, the white crown on its head.

AEGINA
Eleven o'clock, wind on the uphill to Old Chora. Not a soul.

SPETSES
Sti. Anargyri. The luminous seafloor in the shallows full of little holes, and above the pine, old, broken, unloading its fragrance as if paying back an old debt.

HYDRA
Holy Friday. In the boats, priests and boys with cherubim. The crowd with lit candles. O my sweet spring...

PATMOS
The trembling surf pale, and the conical boulder facing it heavy, dark. The *dook-dook* of an unseen motor schooner passing by is heard.

RHODOS
In the old Greek quarter. Whatever the eye can catch from half-open doors: barefoot babies and huge banana leaves. In the background, laundry on the line, a cat.

CYPRUS
In "Sultan Tekeh" just outside Larnaka. Leaf shadows shift rhythmically in the wind and seem a sieve worked ceaselessly just like a conscience.

AIX-EN-PROVENCE
Suddenly spring. Between sculpted railings, a girl's head, looking perplexed.

ST.-JEAN-CAP-FERRAT
The seaside trail leading to Beaulieu. To the left, a huge garden with multiple terraces and a tall dog staring haughtily. To the right the sea, almost white. Smell of fresh cut clover.

PALERMO
Church interior as it appeared in my sleep. Reddish frescoes and, on the floor, black and white tiles. Heat.

AMPURIAS
Autumn afternoon among the ruins. You gaze at the sea, dull in the fine rain, and think about a lost Greek empire. For the sake of language, not anything else.

CÓRDOBA
Diminutive *patio* in a poor neighborhood. Little fountain, arches, openings behind them curtained off with beads. Two shorn boys, full of curiosity, stop their game to observe the stranger.

CONSTANTINOPLE
From the deck of "Felix Dzerdzinsky." A crowd of fierce faces on the pier. Far in the distance, among the minaret spears, Aghia Sofia.

CAIRO
In the dust and crowd of a common quarter. A funeral pro-
cession with Coptic priests whispering incomprehensible
words in the blazing noon.

b

AEGINA
Blend of Hyssop and Jasmine at midnight.

SPETSES
The prow pitching and beating on the waves. Each time,
foamdust, full on the face.

ZAKYNTHOS
Twilight on the Cape, in the old house of Dionysios Solomos.
Silence and awe in front of the large, round, stone, garden
table. And a simultaneous undercurrent of strange comfort.

MYTILENE
A spoonful of blackberry preserves after afternoon sleep.

CHIOS
Pyrgi. From the unbearable heat to the moist interior of the
church. A sensation of whitewash and half-vanished frescoes
the length of the body.

SIFNOS
Room with arches. The naked body as native, you might say,
as when you were born in the solar ossuary.

KALYMNOS
A red snapper broiled with plenty of choice oil and lemon.

C

ANNOULA
As she bathes, having finished the laundry, in the large stone basin of the house. White luminous body.

ALEXANDRA
Who studies for entrance exams while absent-mindedly caressing her left breast and then, using the pencil in her hand, rhythmically embroidering its nipple.

SPERANZA
As the moon advances and captures her feet-first. She floats on her back in its light and, from the rise and fall of her nude breasts, a scent of garden and of sea arrives.

DEMETRA
High on the chimney of the roof. The wind takes hair and dress. Her very skin glows and she turns left and right like a bird, inexplicably happy.

BILLIO
Who lets her nightgown drop, picks it up, discards it finally and sits facing the balcony, her bra unfastened in the back.

INO
At night before sleep. She waters the plants in the strong veranda light, her body outlined under the gauzy nightgown. You confuse her with the flowers.

POPPY, ANGELA, HARIKLEIA
Who sleep deeply: one with her thighs this way; the other's hand on a naked breast; the third's right leg flexed, arms high around her head. While a breeze of bruised violet and lemon tree rounds the door's lip.

[107]

THE

LITTLE

MARINER

[*Spotlight d*]

SCENE ONE : Odysseas Androutsos commands that the emissaries of Areios Pagos, Noutsos and Panourgias, be arrested and executed.

SCENE TWO : A special committee acting as a court martial condemns George Karaiskakis as "menace and traitor to the land."

SCENE THREE : Condemned to death, Theodoros Kolokotronis is thrown in jail.

SCENE FOUR : Sunday morning, in Nauplion, outside the church, Governor Ioannis Kapodistrias falls to the Mavromichaels' bullets.

SCENE FIVE : Leaving the Gare de Lyons, in Paris, after the signing of the Sèvres pact, Eleutherios Venizelos receives the bullets of two Greek officers.

SCENE SIX : Under German occupation, the Greek Popular Liberation Army exterminates Colonel Psaros, who is fighting for the same exact cause as head of an independent guerilla group.

SCENE SEVEN : In Cyprus, men sent by the Dictator government of Athens set a trap for National Leader Makarios, who just manages to escape.

ANOINT THE

ARISTON

[XX–XXVIII]

XXII

SOMETIMES I go into the air as if reading the Iliad. I take the path that leads above the houses, high, and, as cove and embrace change their shape with my ascent, emotions too change place and form in me: the identity of heroes, the savage satisfaction of saying *no,* the direct, the luminous, the never twice the same.

A dark teenager whose undergarment has been lowered and who remains beautiful next to all kinds of indigo and black. Hard to see in Christianity; impossible to find in Marxism; small Alexander the Great over the Aegean he embodies and whose light and surf never end.

XXIII

THE SUN must surely have a childhood as a clear waterdrop. That's why he glimmers in an eyelash; and keeps the coolness on the frescoed Saints, July, high noon.

Not to mention transparency. Which, if luck lets you love a girl, you see within: As in poems.

If it is possible to die without perishing, it must be so: a transparency where your final components – fire, dew – being visible to all, one way or another, you too will exist in perpetua.

XXIV

FOR WHOM THE SEA in the sun is a "landscape" – life seems easy and death as well. But for anyone else it's a reflection of immortality, it is "duration." A duration whose own blinding light prevents you from perceiving.

If it were possible to stand, at the same time, before and after things, you'd see how much time's chasm, which simply devours events, loses its meaning; as in, exactly, a poem. And then – since a poem develops the instantaneous or, conversely, contracts the infinite – one can earn one's freedom without resorting to any kind of explosives.

If we could only understand one thing: that everything isn't held by the living.

X X V

A TRANSLITERATION of the sound achieved by the *paf-flapping* of small surf, while the moon gains distance and the house draws near the shore, could reveal a lot. About the crowns of the senses, for one. Where gentleness, supplanting power, always arrives first: a glowing pistachio-green, the pebble lit, the wind's solitary footsteps on the leaves. Or else: something frontal, a dome, rendering nature linear as the surf's purl turns the Greek tongue ecumenical.

Learn to pronounce reality correctly.

XXVI

PRONOUNCE REALITY as the sparrow does the dawn. And approach it as a ship does Serifos or Milos. Where mountains unfold one from the other until the splendid cone with its white houses is revealed; one island divided in two or three; and the perpendicular boulder is seen, up close, to hold the most virgin white embrace. Profound penetration into the senses and simultaneously constant reversal of any utilitarian concept about the nature of the material world.

Nowhere did I feel my life so justified as on a ship's bridge. Everything in its proper place: sheet-metal, pipes, screws, cables, flotation devices, airshafts; and I myself inscribing the constant transformation by remaining fixed. A full, self-sufficient and organized world that responds to me, and I to it, and together we penetrate miracle and danger as one body.

Enduring ship, my land.

XXVII

I WAS LATE in understanding the meaning of humility, and it's the fault of those who taught me to place it at the other end of pride. You must domesticate the idea of existence in you to understand it.

One day when I was feeling abandoned by everything and a great sorrow fell slowly on my soul, walking across the fields without salvation, I pulled a branch of some unknown bush. I broke it and brought it to my upper lip. I understood immediately that man is innocent. I read it in that truth-acerbic scent so vividly, I took to its road with light step and a missionary heart. Until my deepest conscience was that all religions lie.

Yes, Paradise wasn't nostalgia. Nor, much less, a reward. It was a right.

XXVIII

WE WALK thousands of years. We call the sky "sky" and the sea "sea." All things will change one day and we too with them, but our nature will irretrievably be carved on the geometry we disdained in Plato. And in it, when we bow, as sometimes we bow over the waters of our island, we'll find the same brown hills, inlets and coves, same windmills and the same abandoned chapels, the small houses leaning on each other and the vineyards asleep like children, the dovecots and the domes.

I don't mean these themselves. I mean the soul's same natural and spontaneous movements that generate matter and order it in a specific direction; the same pulses, the same lifting up toward the deeper meaning of a *humble Paradise,* which is our true self, our justice, our freedom, our second and true ethical sun.

BUT INCONCEIVABLY NO
                          one hears. The bird of Paradise
ever flies higher in flames. The voice turns elsewhere,
the eyes stay miracle-free.

Abandoned are the eyes

One among the thousand murderers, I too take the innocent,
the weak. I wrap the ancient garment round me and descend
the stone steps again, calling and exorcising

Abandoned are the eyes you call

eons now over the blue volcanoes. Far in the body, and far in
the soil I stand on, I went to find out who I am. Rich in small
joys and unexpected meetings, look at me: incapable of learn-
ing what I give, what I am given, and still injustice has the
greater part

Gold wind of life . . .

NOTES

Quotations in the Preface are drawn from *The Little Mariner* and from Elytis's essays "First Things First" and "Chronicle of a Decade," currently in translation manuscript.

MARINER : the Greek word is *nautilus,* an archaic form of sailor, with a secondary meaning of the nautilus shell.

SPOTLIGHTS : illustrations of betrayal, injustice, duplicity and persecution through time.

SPOTLIGHT a (pg. 13) : spans a spectrum of time from antiquity to the present. Nauplio: the first capital of Greece, after the liberation of its southern part from the Turks in the 1820s. EAT/ESA are acronyms for Greek military police.

ANOINT THE ARISTON (pg. 15) : the word for anoint is *myrisai,* an archaic form, whose second meaning is to smell; it is the root of the word myrrh. Ariston is the superlative of good. Since John Fowles has a book titled *The Aristos,* and *aristocracy* is a familiar word, I have retained the Greek to parallel the formality and antiquity evoked in the original text by this subtitle.

WITH LIGHT AND WITH DEATH
4 (pg. 30) : Franks: generic term for Latinate and Nordic invaders of Greece, as distinguished from Islamic; by extension, Europeans.
5 (pg. 31) : Pergamos, Miletos: Greek islands; Syrtis, Myrtilla: placenames.
7 (pg. 33) : Mesolonghi: small town on the mainland, to the west of Delphi, where a major battle was fought against the Turks, and where Lord Byron died. The French painter Delacroix has a famous painting drawn from this battle, *Greece Expiring on the Ruins of Mesolonghi.*

WHAT ONE LOVES (pg. 35) : *Otto tis eratai* in the original, in Attic Greek.

SPOTLIGHT b (pg. 47) : all scenes are set in Ancient Greece. Miltiades: com-
    manding general in the battle of Marathon, 490 B.C. Aristeides:
    general of the same time, known as Aristeides the Just, famed for
    his logic and lack of personal ambition. The Thirty: junta of tyrants.
    Pheidias: sculptor of the 5th century B.C., particularly known for
    his work on the Parthenon and the gold and ivory statues of Athena
    and Zeus. Phokion: Athenian general and statesman.

ANOINT THE ARISTON

I X (pg. 52) : pelago: small sea with islands.

X I (pg. 54) : Armstrong: the astronaut.

X I I (pg. 55) : consubstantial: *homoousios,* term taken from the Greek Ortho-
    dox credo, applicable to Jesus, who is believed to be of one and the
    same substance as God, his father, in opposition to the *homoioou-*
    sian belief that the son is essentially like the father but not of the
    same substance. One of the major differences between Orthodox
    and Catholic doctrines.

WITH LIGHT AND WITH DEATH

8 (pg. 61) : in homage to Sappho and the fragmentary nature of most of her
    surviving lyrics. One of several poems in the "With Light and with
    Death" sections that echo or mimic archaic forms.

11 (pg. 64) : written in the style deriving from *boustrophedon,* literally *as the*
    bull turns (in ploughing), in which lines of words in capitals and
    with no breaks between them were inscribed, usually on stone
    stellae, alternately left to right, right to left, left to right. *Boustro-*
    phedon gave way to a left to right style that retained, for a time, the
    lack of spaces between words.

12 (pg. 65) : The Virgin Mary is much loved in Greece, and her shrines and
    chapels are distinguished by a plethora of affectionate, geographi-
    cal, historical or miracle-evoking appellations.

13 (pg. 67) : Sikinos: Aegean island.

WHAT ONE LOVES (pg. 69) : *Aegeodrome*: word-play off the Greek word for airport, *aerodrome,* whose components are air, *aero,* and runway, *drome.* The catalog is richly and sensuously varied in the original by wide use of dialect and regional speech.

SPOTLIGHT C (pg. 79) : set in Byzantium.

ANOINT THE ARISTON

X V I I (pg. 85) : Hegeso, St. Ecaterine: place-names.

X I X (pg. 87) : blisses: Greek has a word, *hedone,* root of hedonism in English, that encompasses the specific sensations leading to and culminating in orgasm. The French call it *jouissance.*

X X I (pg. 89) : Hermes, leg flexed: it was a significant breakthrough in the history of Greek sculpture to separate the legs, flexing one of them, thus giving the figure fluidity, subtlety, and engagement from any perspective, compared to earlier works that had primarily frontal appeal.

WITH LIGHT AND WITH DEATH

15 (pg. 93) : Aegina: Aegean island; Mytilene: capital of Lesbos, a large Aegean island, where Elytis's family is from and where he lived, in part, as a child.

17 (pg. 95) : this poem is written in Ancient Greek in the original. I have tried to retain some of the formality and stately cadence made possible by its intricate syntax. Kore: literally, daughter, young woman; female of a type of early Greek statue, the Kouros, characterized by a frontal approach, arms joined to the sides of the body, legs joined to each other, and a consistent, haunting, very beautiful enigmatic smile.

19 (pg. 97) : Psara: place-name.

20 (pg. 98) : this poem does not have a literal coherent meaning in the original. Its appeal is lyrical, emotional, a breakdown of speech in the face of (what I interpret as) a call from the other side.

21 (pg. 99) : Horn-head: translation of *Keratios,* proper name from the root *keras,* horn; it suggests both Devil and cuckold, deceiver and deceived.

THE SNAPSHOTS (pg. 101) : in Greek, the word for snapshot, *stigmiotypon*, is composed of the words *stigme*, moment, and *typos*, print, or a type. The poet puns on this in "I'd wrested types from moments."

a : place-names here refer to islands, and seaside or riverside cities.

b : place-names refer to Greek islands.

Solomos: Greek poet, author of the Greek national anthem.

SPOTLIGHT d (pg. 111) : scenes 1–3 are drawn from the successful battle for independence against the Turks in the 1820s. Androutsos, Karais-kakis and Kolokotronis are heroes of this revolution.

Aerios Pagos is the Greek Supreme Court; it has retained its name from antiquity to the present.

Kapodistrias: first governor of free Greece; the Mavromichaels led a mutiny against him in 1831, and, after killing him, perished themselves.

Venizelos: early twentieth-century statesman.

Makarios: Archbishop Makarios, National Leader of Cyprus, whom the military junta of 1967 attempted to assassinate; this failed attempt led to their downfall shortly thereafter.

TRANSLATOR'S ACKNOWLEDGMENTS

I would like to thank Jane Miller for her untiring critical, grammatical, and lucid presence. And Rita Speicher, Carolyn Forché and Tree Swenson for close readings of the manuscript. Finally, my mother, Claire Broumas, my willing liaison in Greece.

This translation is dedicated to Tree Swenson.